# The Data Breach

*How Cybersecurity Threats and Privacy Risks Impact Millions of Mobile Line Customers and What You Need to Know to Protect Yourself*

**Martha Belony**

Copyright © 2024 Martha Belony

All rights reserved. No part of this publication may be reproduced, distributed, or transmitted in any form or by any means, including photocopying, recording, or other electronic or mechanical methods, without the prior written permission of the publisher, except in the case of brief quotations embodied in critical reviews and certain other noncommercial uses permitted by copyright law

# Table of Contents

**Introduction**

**Chapter 1**

The Breach Unveiled

**Chapter 2**

Understanding Metadata

**Chapter 3**

Risks and Threats

**Chapter 4**

Customer Responses and Concerns

**Chapter 5**

Legal and Regulatory Landscape

**Chapter 6**

Protecting Yourself Online

# Introduction

The AT&T data breach of 2022 stands as one of the most significant cybersecurity incidents in recent history. Affecting nearly all of AT&T's 110 million wireless subscribers and those of other providers using its network, this breach exposed the call data of millions of Americans. The breach period, spanning from May 1, 2022, to October 31, 2022, saw an illegal download of data from a third-party cloud platform that included metadata such as call logs. These logs detailed every number AT&T customers called or texted, the frequency of interactions, and the duration of calls.

AT&T discovered the breach in April 2023, amidst dealing with another unrelated major data leak. The breach not only compromised the privacy of millions but also highlighted the vulnerabilities in data management and security practices among major telecom providers. Although no names, addresses, or Social Security numbers were stolen, the compromised metadata is significant. Such data can be used to infer relationships and patterns of communication, making it a valuable asset for cybercriminals. For instance, hackers could use this information to craft more convincing phishing attacks, posing as trusted contacts or institutions.

The breach has severe implications. Cybercriminals can now identify who communicates frequently with which numbers, providing them with an edge in social engineering attacks. For example, if a hacker notices a customer frequently contacting a bank, they could craft a targeted phishing attempt posing as the bank. This kind of information is particularly dangerous when coupled with advancements in artificial intelligence, which can create convincing deepfakes and other sophisticated scams.

The exposure of cell tower ID numbers in the breach further exacerbates the risk. These IDs can help bad actors track geolocations, making it easier for them to conduct targeted attacks or surveillance. This breach has underscored the need for robust cybersecurity measures and heightened awareness among consumers about potential threats.

In response to the breach, cybersecurity experts have emphasized the importance of vigilance among AT&T customers. They advise customers to be particularly cautious about unsolicited calls or texts asking for sensitive information. It is recommended to verify any suspicious communications by directly contacting the supposed sender through known and trusted channels.

This breach is a stark reminder of the fragile nature of digital security in today's interconnected world. It raises critical questions about the adequacy of current cybersecurity practices and the role of regulatory bodies in enforcing stringent data protection measures. The responsibility for safeguarding data extends beyond individuals to the corporations that collect and manage vast amounts of personal information. This incident highlights the urgent need for stronger regulations and oversight to prevent such breaches in the future and protect the privacy and security of millions of users.

In the digital age, data privacy and cybersecurity have emerged as critical issues affecting individuals, businesses, and governments worldwide. The AT&T data breach is a poignant example of the vulnerabilities that exist and the far-reaching consequences of failing to protect sensitive information. Data privacy refers to the right of individuals to control their personal information and how it is collected, used, and shared. Cybersecurity encompasses the measures and practices designed to protect data from unauthorized access, theft, and damage.

The importance of data privacy cannot be overstated. Personal data, ranging from contact information to financial records, is highly valuable. When this data falls into the wrong hands, it can lead to identity theft, financial loss, and a breach of personal security. The AT&T data breach exposed not only the call logs and communication patterns of millions of users but also highlighted the potential for misuse of such information in phishing attacks and other forms of cybercrime.

Cybersecurity is equally crucial. It involves the implementation of technologies, processes, and controls to protect systems, networks, and data from cyber attacks. Effective cybersecurity measures ensure the confidentiality, integrity, and availability of data, protecting it from malicious actors. In the case of AT&T, the breach revealed significant lapses in their cybersecurity protocols, particularly in safeguarding data stored on third-party platforms. This incident underscores the necessity for companies to adopt robust cybersecurity frameworks and regularly update them to counter evolving threats.

The consequences of inadequate cybersecurity and data privacy measures are manifold. For individuals, breaches can lead to financial loss, emotional distress, and a loss of trust in digital services. For businesses, the repercussions include reputational damage, legal liabilities, and significant financial losses. The AT&T breach, for instance, has likely eroded customer trust and could result in costly legal battles and regulatory fines.

Furthermore, the breach has broader implications for society. It highlights the interconnected nature of modern digital infrastructure, where a vulnerability in one system can have cascading effects on others. As more services and devices become interconnected, the potential attack surface for cybercriminals expands, necessitating a coordinated and comprehensive approach to cybersecurity.

Governments and regulatory bodies play a pivotal role in ensuring data privacy and cybersecurity. They must establish and enforce stringent data protection laws and standards, mandate regular security audits, and hold companies accountable for breaches. Public awareness and education are also vital. Individuals need to be informed about the risks and best practices for protecting their data, such as using strong passwords, enabling multi-factor authentication, and being wary of phishing attempts.

The AT&T data breach serves as a wake-up call for the importance of data privacy and cybersecurity. It underscores the need for proactive measures to protect personal information and the critical role of both individuals and organizations in safeguarding data. As cyber threats continue to evolve, a collective effort is required to build a secure digital environment that upholds the privacy and security of all users.

# Chapter 1: The Breach Unveiled

In April 2023, AT&T, one of the largest telecommunications providers in the United States, publicly disclosed a significant data breach that compromised the privacy of millions of its customers. The breach, which occurred between May 1, 2022, and October 31, 2022, was discovered during a routine security audit, revealing unauthorized access to sensitive customer data stored on a third-party cloud platform. This discovery sent shockwaves through the cybersecurity community and raised serious concerns about data protection practices within the telecommunications industry.

The timeline of events surrounding the AT&T data breach is crucial to understanding its magnitude and implications. The breach itself spanned over a six-month period, beginning in May 2022 and continuing until October 2022. During this time, cybercriminals exploited a vulnerability in a third-party cloud service provider utilized by AT&T, gaining unauthorized access to extensive datasets containing metadata from AT&T's cellular customers.

AT&T first became aware of the breach in early April 2023, when cybersecurity teams conducting routine audits detected unusual activity within their network. Upon further investigation, it was revealed that call logs and metadata from nearly all of AT&T's 110 million wireless subscribers had been accessed without authorization. This data included detailed records of calls made and received, text messages sent and received, call durations, and even some customers' cell tower ID numbers.

The discovery of the breach triggered an immediate response from AT&T's executive team and cybersecurity personnel. The company swiftly launched an internal investigation to assess the extent of the data exposure and identify the specific vulnerabilities that were exploited. Concurrently, AT&T began notifying affected customers and regulatory authorities about the breach, in accordance with legal requirements and industry best practices.

As news of the breach spread, it attracted widespread media attention and scrutiny from cybersecurity experts, consumer advocates, and government officials alike. Questions were raised about AT&T's data security practices, including its oversight of third-party vendors and the adequacy of its response mechanisms to mitigate such incidents. The timing of the breach discovery, coinciding with another unrelated major data leak, further intensified public concern and underscored the vulnerabilities inherent in digital data management.

The scope and impact of the AT&T data breach on its customers cannot be overstated. With approximately 110 million wireless subscribers as of the end of 2022, the breach affected nearly every AT&T customer during the specified timeframe. While AT&T clarified that no names, addresses, or Social Security numbers were compromised, the exposure of metadata posed significant risks to customer privacy and security.

Metadata, such as call logs and communication patterns, provides valuable insights into individuals' behavior and relationships. For cybercriminals, this information can be leveraged to orchestrate targeted phishing attacks, impersonate trusted entities, or even facilitate identity theft. By analyzing call durations, frequency of contacts, and cell tower ID numbers, malicious actors can build detailed profiles of individuals and their interactions, potentially leading to further exploitation of personal information.

Furthermore, the breach exposed vulnerabilities in AT&T's network infrastructure and third-party data management practices. The unauthorized access to sensitive customer data underscored gaps in cybersecurity defenses, raising concerns about the adequacy of safeguards in place to protect against sophisticated cyber threats. As a result, affected customers were left vulnerable to potential exploitation and faced heightened risks of falling victim to fraud or other malicious activities.

In response to the breach, AT&T took immediate steps to enhance its cybersecurity posture and mitigate further risks to customer data. The company collaborated with cybersecurity experts and regulatory authorities to implement remedial measures, including strengthening network security protocols, enhancing monitoring capabilities, and reviewing its relationships with third-party vendors. Additionally, AT&T provided affected customers with guidance on how to safeguard their personal information and offered identity theft protection services as a precautionary measure.

The fallout from the breach extended beyond immediate remediation efforts. It prompted broader discussions about data privacy, regulatory oversight, and corporate responsibility in safeguarding consumer information. Government officials called for stricter regulations governing data security practices among telecommunications providers, emphasizing the need for transparency, accountability, and proactive measures to prevent future breaches.

For AT&T customers, the breach served as a stark reminder of the vulnerabilities inherent in digital communication and the critical importance of exercising caution in sharing personal information online. It underscored the need for individuals to remain vigilant against phishing scams, unauthorized solicitations, and other forms of cyber threats targeting their personal data. Moreover, the incident highlighted the evolving nature of cybersecurity threats and the ongoing challenges faced by companies in protecting sensitive customer information in an increasingly interconnected world.

The AT&T data breach of 2022-2023 revealed significant lapses in data security practices and raised fundamental questions about the protection of consumer privacy in the digital age. By examining the timeline of events and assessing the scope of its impact on AT&T customers, it becomes clear that robust cybersecurity measures and proactive risk management are essential to safeguarding sensitive data and maintaining public trust in telecommunications services.

# Chapter 2: Understanding Metadata

Metadata refers to descriptive information about data that provides context, structure, and attributes to the primary data it describes. In the context of telecommunications and digital communications, metadata includes information about the communication itself rather than the content of the communication. For example, in the case of AT&T's data breach, metadata would encompass details such as the numbers dialed or texted, the duration of calls, timestamps, and the frequency of interactions.

Unlike the content of a communication (such as the actual words spoken in a phone call or written in a text message), which is considered substantive data, metadata provides insights into the communication patterns and behaviors of individuals. This distinction is crucial because while metadata does not reveal the specific content of communications, it can still divulge significant information about the parties involved, the frequency of their interactions, and the nature of their relationships.

In the realm of telecommunications, metadata serves several important functions. It helps service providers manage and optimize network traffic, track usage patterns, and bill customers accurately based on their usage. From a user perspective, metadata plays a role in providing call records for billing purposes, identifying missed calls, and enabling features like call forwarding or voicemail notifications.

However, from a privacy and security standpoint, metadata can be highly revealing. It can potentially disclose sensitive information such as who a person communicates with most frequently, the duration and timing of their communications, and their geographic location based on cell tower information. As such, metadata has become a focal point in debates over privacy rights, data protection, and the ethical use of telecommunications data.

Call and text logs, a specific type of metadata, represent a detailed record of an individual's communications over a specified period. These logs typically include information such as phone numbers dialed or received, timestamps of calls and texts, call durations, and in some cases, the location data of the cell tower handling the communication.

The significance of call and text logs lies in their potential to reveal patterns of communication and behavior. For telecommunications providers like AT&T, these logs are essential for operational purposes such as billing, network optimization, and customer service. However, from a privacy perspective, the aggregation and analysis of call and text logs can paint a detailed picture of an individual's social network, habits, and routines.

In the context of cybersecurity and data breaches, the exposure of call and text logs poses significant risks to individuals' privacy and security. Cybercriminals who gain unauthorized access to such data can exploit it for various malicious purposes, including targeted phishing attacks, identity theft, or surveillance. By analyzing call patterns and relationships inferred from metadata, hackers can craft sophisticated social engineering attacks that appear legitimate and convincing to their targets.

Moreover, the revelation of call and text logs can have broader implications for personal and professional relationships. For instance, unauthorized access to communication metadata can compromise the confidentiality of sensitive discussions, expose business dealings, or reveal personal connections that individuals may prefer to keep private.

The potential misuse of call and text logs underscores the importance of robust data protection measures and privacy safeguards. Telecommunications providers and other custodians of metadata have a responsibility to implement stringent security protocols, encryption technologies, and access controls to prevent unauthorized access and mitigate the risks associated with data breaches.

From a regulatory standpoint, the handling of metadata is subject to legal and ethical considerations. In many jurisdictions, laws such as the General Data Protection Regulation (GDPR) in Europe or the California Consumer Privacy Act (CCPA) in the United States impose strict requirements on companies regarding the collection, storage, and use of personal data, including metadata. These regulations aim to protect individuals' privacy rights and ensure that companies adhere to transparent and accountable data practices.

Metadata, particularly in the form of call and text logs, plays a dual role in telecommunications: it is essential for operational efficiency and customer service, yet it also poses significant privacy and security risks. Understanding the nature of metadata, its implications for privacy, and the potential consequences of its exposure is crucial for both consumers and organizations entrusted with safeguarding sensitive data. As technologies evolve and cybersecurity threats become more sophisticated, ongoing vigilance and proactive measures are essential to mitigate risks and uphold the integrity of telecommunications data privacy.

# Chapter 3: Risks and Threats

The potential misuse of breached data, such as the metadata compromised in the AT&T data breach, poses significant risks to individuals and organizations alike. While the breach primarily exposed call and text logs without revealing names, addresses, or Social Security numbers, the implications for privacy and security are profound. Understanding how cybercriminals may exploit this data is crucial to assessing the full extent of the risks involved.

Cybercriminals who gain access to metadata can exploit it in various ways, leveraging the information to perpetrate targeted attacks and fraud schemes. One of the most immediate concerns is the possibility of phishing attacks. Armed with knowledge of whom an individual communicates with frequently, cybercriminals can craft highly convincing phishing messages posing as trusted contacts or institutions. For instance, they may send fraudulent emails or text messages purportedly from a bank, utility provider, or even a friend, requesting sensitive information or prompting the recipient to click on malicious links.

Moreover, the exposure of call and text logs enables cybercriminals to conduct sophisticated social engineering attacks. By analyzing communication patterns and relationships inferred from metadata, attackers can gather intelligence about an individual's social network, professional contacts, and personal relationships. This information can be exploited to tailor scams that exploit trust and familiarity, increasing the likelihood that recipients will fall victim to deception.

Another significant risk associated with the misuse of breached metadata is identity theft. While the AT&T breach did not compromise sensitive personal information such as Social Security numbers, cybercriminals can still use metadata to piece together enough details to impersonate individuals or conduct unauthorized transactions. For example, knowledge of frequent interactions with financial institutions or service providers can facilitate identity fraud attempts, where attackers attempt to assume the identity of the victim for financial gain or other malicious purposes.

Furthermore, the exposure of call and text logs can have implications for personal safety and security. Cybercriminals armed with location data obtained from cell tower IDs can potentially track individuals' movements and whereabouts. This information can be particularly concerning in cases where individuals, such as public figures or high-profile individuals, may be targeted for harassment, surveillance, or physical harm based on their identifiable patterns of communication and location data.

From a broader societal perspective, the misuse of breached metadata contributes to erosion of trust in digital communication channels and telecommunications providers. Customers who entrust their data to service providers rightfully expect that their privacy will be protected and that adequate security measures are in place to prevent unauthorized access. When breaches occur and sensitive information is compromised, it undermines confidence in the security practices of the affected organization and raises concerns about the vulnerability of personal data in an increasingly digital world.

The cybersecurity implications of the AT&T data breach extend beyond the immediate impact on affected customers to encompass broader systemic vulnerabilities and regulatory considerations. The breach highlighted shortcomings in data security practices and underscored the challenges faced by telecommunications providers in safeguarding sensitive customer information from sophisticated cyber threats.

Firstly, the breach underscored the need for robust cybersecurity frameworks and proactive threat detection mechanisms within telecommunications companies. Effective cybersecurity measures, such as encryption of sensitive data, multifactor authentication, and regular security audits, are essential to mitigate the risk of unauthorized access and data breaches. By investing in advanced security technologies and implementing best practices, organizations can enhance their resilience against evolving cyber threats and protect customer data from exploitation.

Secondly, the AT&T breach raised concerns about regulatory oversight and compliance with data protection laws. In the aftermath of the breach, regulatory authorities may scrutinize the company's adherence to privacy regulations and impose penalties for non-compliance. Regulations such as the General Data Protection Regulation (GDPR) in Europe and the California Consumer Privacy Act (CCPA) in the United States impose strict requirements on organizations regarding the collection, storage, and use of personal data, including metadata. Compliance with these regulations is not only a legal obligation but also a critical component of maintaining trust and accountability with customers.

Moreover, the cybersecurity implications of the breach highlight the interconnected nature of global data ecosystems and the need for international cooperation in combating cyber threats. Cybercriminals operate across borders, exploiting vulnerabilities in digital infrastructure to target organizations and individuals worldwide. Collaborative efforts between governments, law enforcement agencies, and private sector stakeholders are essential to develop coordinated responses to cyber incidents, share threat intelligence, and strengthen global cybersecurity resilience.

From a corporate governance perspective, the AT&T breach underscores the importance of transparency and proactive communication with stakeholders in the event of a data breach. Timely and accurate disclosure of breaches, along with clear guidance on remedial actions and risk mitigation strategies, is essential to maintain public trust and demonstrate commitment to customer welfare. By adopting a proactive approach to cybersecurity incident response and prioritizing customer protection, organizations can mitigate reputational damage and minimize the financial and operational impacts of data breaches.

The risks and threats associated with the potential misuse of breached metadata, as exemplified by the AT&T data breach, underscore the critical importance of robust cybersecurity measures, regulatory compliance, and proactive risk management strategies. By addressing vulnerabilities in data security practices, enhancing regulatory oversight, and fostering international cooperation, organizations can mitigate the impact of cyber threats and safeguard sensitive customer information in an increasingly interconnected digital landscape. As technology continues to evolve and cyber threats become more sophisticated, continuous vigilance and investment in cybersecurity resilience are essential to protect against emerging risks and uphold trust in digital communications.

# Chapter 4: Customer Responses and Concerns

The revelation of a significant data breach affecting AT&T customers prompted immediate responses from both the telecommunications giant and regulatory bodies tasked with overseeing data privacy and consumer protection. The initial reactions from AT&T and regulatory bodies set the stage for understanding the severity of the breach, its implications for affected customers, and the measures taken to address the situation.

Upon discovering the data breach, AT&T moved swiftly to investigate the incident and assess the extent of the compromise. In its initial public statements, AT&T acknowledged that data from "nearly all" of its cellular customers and customers of wireless providers using its network between May 1, 2022, and October 31, 2022, had been breached. The company attributed the breach to an "illegal download" on a third-party cloud platform, which it became aware of in April. This disclosure came amidst another major data leak incident that AT&T was concurrently managing, underscoring the complexity and scale of the cybersecurity challenges faced by the company.

From a regulatory standpoint, AT&T's response also involved notifying appropriate authorities and cooperating with investigations to determine the root cause of the breach and mitigate its impact. The company emphasized its commitment to transparency and accountability, pledging to provide affected customers with information about the breach and steps they could take to protect themselves against potential risks.

Regulatory bodies responsible for overseeing data privacy and consumer protection, such as the Federal Trade Commission (FTC) in the United States and relevant authorities in other jurisdictions, responded promptly to the AT&T data breach. These regulatory bodies play a crucial role in enforcing compliance with data protection laws and holding organizations accountable for safeguarding consumer information.

In response to the breach, regulatory bodies typically initiate investigations to assess whether AT&T adhered to data protection regulations and whether adequate safeguards were in place to prevent unauthorized access to customer data. Depending on the findings of these investigations, regulatory bodies may impose fines, penalties, or other corrective actions to address any deficiencies in AT&T's data security practices.

The public and customer responses to the AT&T data breach reflected a mix of concern, frustration, and calls for greater accountability in data protection. For affected customers, the breach raised immediate concerns about the security of their personal information and the potential risks of identity theft, fraud, or other malicious activities. Many customers expressed dismay over the breach's scope and the implications for their privacy rights, emphasizing the need for stronger data security measures and transparency from telecommunications providers.

In response to the breach, customers sought reassurance from AT&T regarding the steps being taken to mitigate risks and protect their data moving forward. Public statements and communications from AT&T aimed to address customer concerns, providing guidance on how affected individuals could monitor their accounts for suspicious activity and take proactive steps to enhance their cybersecurity posture.

Moreover, the AT&T data breach sparked broader discussions about the adequacy of current data protection regulations and the responsibilities of corporations in safeguarding consumer information. Calls for stricter regulatory oversight and enhanced cybersecurity standards gained traction among consumer advocacy groups, policymakers, and cybersecurity experts, highlighting the need for comprehensive reforms to protect individuals' privacy rights in the digital age.

The initial reactions from AT&T and regulatory bodies, coupled with public and customer responses, underscored the significant impact of the data breach on affected individuals and the broader implications for data privacy and cybersecurity. By addressing the immediate concerns of customers, cooperating with regulatory investigations, and enhancing data security measures, AT&T sought to restore trust and demonstrate its commitment to protecting customer information. Moving forward, the aftermath of the breach serves as a catalyst for strengthening cybersecurity resilience, improving regulatory frameworks, and advancing efforts to safeguard consumer data against evolving cyber threats. As organizations and policymakers continue to grapple with the challenges of data breaches and cybersecurity vulnerabilities, proactive measures and collaborative approaches are essential to mitigate risks and uphold trust in digital communications.

# Chapter 5: Legal and Regulatory Landscape

In the wake of significant data breaches like the one experienced by AT&T, understanding the legal and regulatory landscape governing data protection is crucial. Data protection laws and regulations aim to safeguard individuals' privacy rights and impose obligations on organizations to secure sensitive information from unauthorized access and breaches. Examining the current legal framework provides insights into the measures in place to address data breaches and the challenges faced in enforcing cybersecurity standards effectively.

In the United States, data protection laws are fragmented, with regulations varying across states and industries. At the federal level, the Health Insurance Portability and Accountability Act (HIPAA) governs the protection of health information, while the Gramm-Leach-Bliley Act (GLBA) regulates financial institutions' handling of consumer data. Additionally, the Children's Online Privacy Protection Act (COPPA) protects children's online privacy.

However, comprehensive federal legislation for general data protection, akin to the European Union's General Data Protection Regulation (GDPR), does not exist in the U.S. States like California have enacted their own stringent laws, such as the California Consumer Privacy Act (CCPA), which grants consumers rights over their personal data and imposes obligations on businesses handling such data.

Internationally, the GDPR sets a global benchmark for data protection standards. It mandates stringent requirements for organizations processing personal data of EU residents, including obligations for data breach notification, consent management, and data subject rights. The GDPR's extraterritorial scope means that companies worldwide must comply if they handle EU citizens' data, significantly influencing global data protection practices.

Challenges in Enforcing Cybersecurity Standards:

Enforcing cybersecurity standards presents several challenges rooted in the complexity of digital ecosystems, evolving cyber threats, and regulatory fragmentation:

- Lack of Uniformity: The absence of a unified federal data protection law in the U.S. results in a patchwork of state laws, complicating compliance efforts for businesses operating across multiple jurisdictions. This fragmented approach hinders consistent enforcement and may lead to regulatory arbitrage.

- Technological Advancements: Rapid technological advancements outpace regulatory frameworks, making it challenging to establish clear guidelines for emerging technologies like artificial intelligence (AI), Internet of Things (IoT), and blockchain. Regulators struggle to keep pace with evolving cyber threats and innovative data processing methods.

- Resource Constraints: Regulatory bodies often face resource constraints in monitoring compliance and investigating data breaches effectively. Limited funding, staffing shortages, and competing priorities hinder their ability to enforce cybersecurity standards rigorously.

- Global Coordination: Cyber threats are transnational, requiring international cooperation among regulatory bodies to combat cybercrime effectively. Differences in legal frameworks and enforcement practices across jurisdictions complicate cross-border data protection and cybersecurity enforcement efforts.

- Corporate Accountability: Holding corporations accountable for data breaches and non-compliance with cybersecurity standards requires robust enforcement mechanisms and penalties proportionate to the severity of violations. Legal challenges and prolonged litigation processes may deter regulatory actions against non-compliant organizations.

Addressing these challenges necessitates collaborative efforts among policymakers, industry stakeholders, and cybersecurity experts to strengthen regulatory frameworks, enhance enforcement capabilities, and promote cybersecurity best practices. Proactive measures such as regular cybersecurity audits, threat intelligence sharing, and public-private partnerships can bolster resilience against cyber threats and safeguard individuals' privacy rights in an increasingly interconnected digital environment.

Navigating the legal and regulatory landscape of data protection involves understanding the multifaceted challenges in enforcing cybersecurity standards amidst evolving technological landscapes and global cyber threats. By fostering international cooperation, enhancing regulatory frameworks, and promoting corporate accountability, stakeholders can advance efforts to protect consumer data, mitigate risks of data breaches, and uphold trust in digital interactions. As digital transformation accelerates, ongoing adaptation of regulatory frameworks and collaborative initiatives are essential to address emerging cyber threats effectively and ensure robust data protection practices across sectors and borders.

# Chapter 6: Protecting Yourself Online

In an increasingly digital world where data breaches and cyber threats are prevalent, safeguarding personal data is paramount. Adopting best practices for personal data security is essential to protect against unauthorized access, identity theft, and other malicious activities targeting individuals' sensitive information. Understanding these practices and integrating them into daily online habits can significantly enhance cybersecurity resilience and mitigate risks associated with digital interactions.

Personal Data Security Best Practices:

Effective personal data security begins with proactive measures to secure sensitive information and minimize exposure to potential threats. Key best practices include:

- Strong Password Management: Creating strong, unique passwords for each online account and regularly updating them helps prevent unauthorized access. Password managers can simplify password management by securely storing and generating complex passwords.

- Two-Factor Authentication (2FA): Enabling 2FA adds an extra layer of security by requiring a second form of verification, such as a code sent to a mobile device, in addition to a password. This mitigates the risk of unauthorized access even if passwords are compromised.

- Secure Wi-Fi and Network Connections: Using encrypted Wi-Fi networks and virtual private networks (VPNs) when accessing sensitive information enhances data security by protecting data transmissions from interception by unauthorized parties.

- Regular Software Updates: Keeping operating systems, applications, and antivirus software up to date with the latest security patches and updates helps defend against vulnerabilities exploited by cyber attackers.

- Data Encryption: Encrypting sensitive data stored on devices and during transmission ensures that even if intercepted, the information remains unreadable without decryption keys, thereby protecting confidentiality.

- Limited Sharing of Personal Information: Exercising caution when sharing personal information online and with third parties minimizes exposure to potential data breaches and identity theft.

- Privacy Settings and Permissions: Adjusting privacy settings on social media platforms and other online accounts to limit visibility of personal information and control data sharing permissions enhances privacy and reduces risks associated with data exposure.

Steps for Mitigating Phishing and Scam Attempts:

Phishing and scam attempts remain prevalent methods used by cybercriminals to trick individuals into divulging personal information or clicking on malicious links. Mitigating these threats requires awareness and adherence to precautionary measures:

- Recognizing Phishing Attempts: Educating oneself about common phishing tactics, such as unsolicited emails, messages, or phone calls requesting sensitive information or urging immediate action, helps individuals identify and avoid falling victim to phishing scams.

- Verifying Sources: Verifying the legitimacy of communications by contacting organizations directly through official channels or visiting their authenticated websites before responding to requests for personal information or clicking on links embedded in suspicious messages.

- Avoiding Clicking on Suspicious Links: Refraining from clicking on links or downloading attachments from unfamiliar or suspicious sources reduces the risk of malware infections or phishing attacks aimed at stealing personal data.

- Suspicious Communication Handling: Exercising caution when receiving unexpected communications claiming urgent action required, financial incentives, or threats, and independently verifying their authenticity before taking any action.

- Reporting Suspected Scams: Promptly reporting suspected phishing attempts or scam activities to relevant authorities, such as consumer protection agencies, financial institutions, or cybersecurity experts, helps prevent further victimization and facilitates investigations into fraudulent activities.

By integrating these best practices into everyday online activities and remaining vigilant against evolving cyber threats, individuals can significantly enhance their personal data security posture and reduce vulnerabilities to cyber attacks. Empowering oneself with knowledge about cybersecurity risks and proactive measures strengthens resilience against data breaches, phishing attempts, and other malicious activities targeting personal information. Ultimately, prioritizing personal data security contributes to safeguarding privacy, maintaining digital trust, and promoting safe online interactions in today's interconnected digital landscape.

www.ingramcontent.com/pod-product-compliance
Lightning Source LLC
Chambersburg PA
CBHW082240220526
45479CB00005B/1293